POLLY, PETE AND PIXIE VISIT THE DOCTOR

Story by Mario Covi
Illustrated by Hildrun Covi

Published by Peter Haddock Ltd, UK for
DERRYDALE BOOKS
NEW YORK

Today is a gray, rainy day. The weather is so bad that Polly, Pete, and Pixie have to play inside the house. Polly has taken Pete's lollipop and he is shouting and running after her. Pixie thinks that this is a new game and chases after the children.

"Don't get so wild," shouts Mom, but the children don't hear her. Then, poor Pixie traps her paw in the door and she is limping on three legs.

Mom says, "Pixie's leg might be broken, we must take her to see the veterinarian."

The waiting room is full. Pixie is sitting on Polly's knee and is feeling very sorry for herself. Polly looks around sadly at all the sick and injured animals. How many different animals can you see? Polly is annoyed with Pete and says, "It's all your fault, you and your lollipop."

Pete replies, "But you took it in the first place!" Mom tells them to be quiet.

Then, the door opens and the veterinarian calls, "Next patient please."

The veterinarian examines Pixie. Carefully, he feels the injured leg, as he talks soothingly to the little dog. Pixie is very frightened. Then she realizes that the veterinarian is a friendly man and is going to help her.

"Yes, the bone is broken," says the veterinarian, "I will put a plaster cast on it, then she'll be able to run around again."

A few weeks later, Mom notices that Polly is very pale and listless. She doesn't want her breakfast. Pete is just the opposite, his plate is nearly empty and he is still hungry.

"Polly doesn't look well," says Dad.

Mom puts her hand on Polly's forehead and says, "She has a temperature."

"My throat is so sore I can't swallow," Polly tells them.

Polly is ill so Mom takes her to the doctor.

Polly, Pete, and Pixie get into the car. When they arrive at the doctor's office, Pete and Pixie stay in the car.

"Watch Pixie and make sure she doesn't chew her plaster cast," Mom tells Pete.

Polly and her Mom sit in the waiting room until their name is called. Then they go in to see the doctor. Polly sits down and the doctor listens to her chest with a stethoscope. Polly is told to breathe deeply. Then, the doctor tells her to open her mouth and say "Aaah" so that she can see Polly's sore throat.

"You have tonsilitis, Polly," says the doctor and tells her to stay in bed for a few days. The doctor gives Mom a prescription for some medicine that will make Polly's throat better.

Polly, Pete and Pixie go with Mom to the drug store. In the shop there is every kind of medicine you could think of for all sorts of illnesses.

The druggist brings the medicine for Polly. As he looks over the counter he sees Pixie's plaster cast.

"Is the whole family ill?" he asks. "No, I'M not," says Pete cheerfully. "Could I have a lollipop?"

Mom scolds him for being rude but the druggist just laughs.

"For you, I have something much better," he says and gives them some candy.

Polly doesn't really want hers so she gives it to Pete when they are outside the shop.

Polly has been in bed for three days. She doesn't have a temperature now but her throat is still sore. Polly has taken her medicine regularly and will soon feel well again.

Pete is bored. He asks Mom if he can stay to talk to Polly.

"No, you can't, Polly is not feeling well."

Pete can't play with Pixie either. The little dog is in her basket. She is sulking because she is not allowed to chew her plaster cast.

Soon Polly is well again and Pixie no longer has to wear her plaster cast.

At night, before the children go to bed, Mom tells them to brush their teeth. Polly never forgets to brush hers but Pete doesn't like it at all.

"I think brushing your teeth is silly," he shouts.

That makes Polly mad. "I have eaten some candy, that's why I'm cleaning them."

Dad has often told Polly that sweet, sugary things are bad for your teeth.

Pete still teases Polly and she splashes him with some water.

From downstairs, Dad shouts, "I can hear what is going on, get into bed now!"

Pete has a toothache. He rubs his cheek, hoping to make the pain go away.

"That's why we have to brush our teeth every morning and every night," says Mom.

Pete starts to cry.

"I think we had better visit the dentist," she says to Pete.

Polly is lucky because her teeth are healthy and strong. She has always looked after them.

Pete says he will always look after his teeth now.

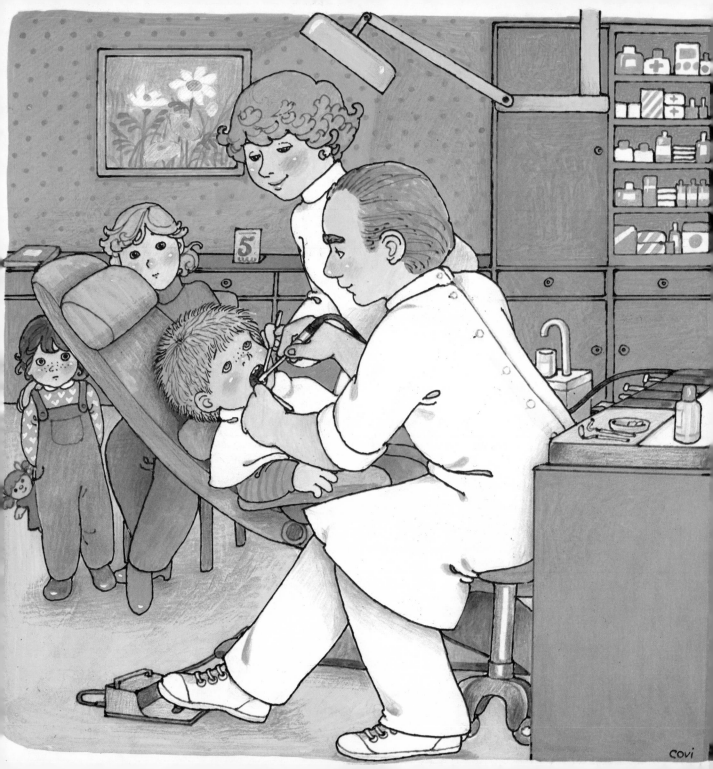